P9-DWX-439

WHEELS

Cars, cogs, carousels, and other things that spin

Words by Tracey Turner   Art by Fatti Burke

WHEELS

Cars, cogs, carousels, and other things that spin

Words by Tracey Turner   Art by Fatti Burke

KINGFISHER
LONDON & NEW YORK

A Raspberry Book
Editorial: Kath Jewitt
Art Direction: Sidonie Beresford-Browne
Cover design: Sidonie Beresford-Browne
Internal design: Peter Clayman
Consultant: Jack Challoner

KINGFISHER
LONDON & NEW YORK

Text and design copyright © Raspberry Books Ltd. 2019
Artwork copyright © Macmillan Publishers International. Ltd 2019
First published 2019 in the United States by Kingfisher
120 Broadway, New York, NY 10271
Kingfisher is an imprint of Macmillan Children's Books, London
All rights reserved

Distributed in the United States and Canada by Macmillan,
120 Broadway, New York, NY 10271

Library of Congress Cataloging-in-Publication data has been applied for.

ISBN 978-0-7534-7531-7

Kingfisher books are available for special promotions and premiums. For details contact:
Special Markets Department, Macmillan, 120 Broadway, New York, NY 10271

For more information, please visit:
www.kingfisherbooks.com

Printed in China
9 8 7 6 5 4 3 2 1
1TR/0819/WKT/UG/128MA

Contents

Landing would be a lot easier with wheels!

Introduction

Wheels are the work of genius, and they have completely changed the world. You might have found them useful on wheelchairs, bikes, buses, trains, cars, and planes. They move things around for us in trucks and wheelbarrows. They make pottery and spin cloth. They fit together as gears to make all kinds of machines work, and they set the first clocks ticking.

As well as being useful, wheels are fun.
They whiz us around on roller-coasters, carousels,
Ferris wheels, roller skates, skateboards, and scooters.
And if you think you'd be bored without wheels,
just imagine how pet hamsters would feel.

Life would be dull without Wheeeels!

But wheels haven't always been around, and they were difficult to invent. There aren't any wheels in the natural world to give people the idea, so making a disk with a hole in the middle and a rod going through it—a wheel and axle—was an amazingly clever idea. In some parts of the world, wheels were never invented: in the Americas, people managed without wheels completely, except for on toys in ancient Mexico.

So let's give the inventor of the wheel an absolutely huge round of applause. Then climb aboard, buckle up your seat belt, and perhaps put on a safety helmet, just in case. It's time to discover the wonder of wheels.

Find out what the world's largest vehicle has in common with the Statue of Liberty.

Learn how to ride downhill on a high-wheel bike.

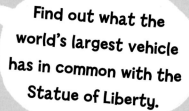

Discover some of the most useful, fun, and unusual wheels in the world!

Potters' Wheels

Potters' wheels were the very first wheels of all. Even before they moved carts, wheels were used to make pots.

Pottery was made by coiling strips of clay and pressing them together—until potters realized that things would be a lot easier if the pot could be spun around. The first potters' wheels, invented around 6,500 years ago, were movable platforms that were turned by hand.

By about 5,000 years ago, potters' wheels could be turned by a second wheel, which was operated with the foot. The wheels spun much more quickly, so potters could throw a lump of clay onto the wheel and use their fingers to shape the pot.

The faster wheels were a breakthrough, because now a lot of pots could be made to the same design in a short length of time—as long as the potter was skilled enough.

Modern potters can use a wheel powered by an electric motor, but some prefer to use human power, just like potters thousands of years ago.

Clay Babies
In ancient Egypt, Khnum was the god of the source of the Nile River. People believed he made human children on a potter's wheel, out of clay taken from the river bed.

It looks a lot easier than it is!

Even gigantic pots can be made on a wheel, though the biggest ones have to be made in sections. Pots like the one below were made in Athens, Greece, more than 2,000 years ago. An artist used liquid clay to add the beautiful decorations.

The First Wheels

No one knows who invented the wheel for transportation, or even where it was invented. But thank goodness someone did.

Before there were wheels, moving heavy objects around was tiring and troublesome. Things were dragged along on sleds, which was hard work.

The earliest transportation wheels ever found are around 5,500 years old and come from central Europe and western Asia.

Ooof! Whew!

Why didn't we think of this BEFORE we built that enormous stone circle?

If the object was pushed and pulled along on top of logs laid next to one another, which rolled as the object moved forward, it made the task a little easier.

Ready to Roll

Putting logs underneath a heavy load keeps the load off the ground. When you push or pull the load, the logs roll. You can achieve the same result by attaching a wheel to an axle, and the axle to a cart that carries the load. And it's much better, because you don't have to keep moving the logs to the front once the object has passed over them.

The wheel and axle meant that people and their possessions could get around on carts pulled by horses or oxen. Now, people could travel and trade much more easily.

The first wheels were made of solid wood. Then someone had another bright idea—by adding spokes, wheels would be much lighter but still strong.

Chariots

⊛ ⊛ ⊛

Ancient chariots raced along on two spoked wheels, pulled by two or more horses. They were light and superfast— and originally made for war.

Chariot wheels need flat ground, so soldiers mounted on horses eventually became more common in battle. Chariots were used for fun instead—chariot racing was one of the events in the Olympic Games of ancient Greece.

Out of my way!

The biggest chariot battle ever was the Battle of Kadesh. fought between the Egyptians and the Hittites in 1274 B.C. Between five and six thousand chariots took part.

The ancient Romans absolutely loved chariot racing. The Circus Maximus in ancient Rome was a huge chariot-racing track, or hippodrome, that could seat 150,000 spectators.

The chariots, driven by professional charioteers, hurtled around the corners and jostled for position. Accidents were common, and charioteers and horses were often seriously injured or killed.

In ancient Rome, charioteers were divided into teams, and the teams could buy and sell them—just like sports teams trade players today. Spectators cheered on their teams with the same enthusiasm as today's sports fans, and rivalry could be fierce.

Charioteers were usually slaves. Winning charioteers could become famous.

Horses could become famous, too!

Circus seats were free in the Roman Empire, although wealthy people could pay for seats with shade and a good view. The emperor had his own entrance to the Circus Maximus, directly connected to his palace.

Waterwheels

Around 2,300 years ago, waterwheels were the first machines to use something other than human or animal power. They harnessed the power of flowing water to do all kinds of useful jobs.

There are different types of waterwheels. This one is driven by water that flows down onto the wheel from the pipe above it.

Wheel made of wood or metal

Axle, which can be connected to other machinery with gears

Paddles or buckets arranged evenly around the outside of the wheel

Waterwheels are so useful because the energy in the turning wheel can be used to power other machinery, usually by a series of gears. Waterwheels can be used for . . .

- Lifting water, perhaps from a river to a field, to water crops
- Turning a big stone mill wheel, which grinds grain to make flour
- Driving bellows for forges and furnaces
- Mushing wood into pulp to make paper
- Driving pumps to keep mines dry (the ancient Romans used waterwheels in mines, including copper mines in Spain and a gold mine in Wales)

Some waterwheels are still turning today. The Laxley Wheel on the Isle of Man, in the British Isles, is the biggest one in the world that is still used—it measures more than 72 feet (22 meters) across!

The modern equivalent of a waterwheel is the water turbine, which is used to generate electricity.

Thanks to wheels, we can all eat the bread made from this flour!

Cogs and Gears

Gears are wheels with teeth, called cogs, around the outside. The cogs of one gear fit together with cogs of another gear, and together they can make all kinds of useful machines.

If you turn this big gear, the smaller gear turns, too, but in the opposite direction. So if the bigger gear turns clockwise, the smaller one will turn counter clockwise. The smaller gear will turn more quickly than the bigger gear.

How fast the small gear goes depends on the number of cogs! Neat, huh?

Gears can increase either speed or force, but not both.
A large gear driving a small gear increases speed.
A small gear driving a big gear increases force.

Gears can be put together in different combinations, and we use them every day. Bikes use gears attached to chains to increase the speed or force provided by the person pedaling. Cars use gears to increase the speed or force provided by the engine. Gears are used in all kinds of ways—in machines in factories, as well as in things that move.

Clockwork uses gears. Someone winds the key to provide the energy, then the energy is stored in a spring. Gears control how the energy is released—to move the hands on a clock, or to make a windup toy move.

Load-lifting Wheels
Wheels are also used in pulleys—
a rope wound around a wheel
with a grooved edge. Pulleys
help lift heavy loads.

Spinning Wheels

Wheels not only got people moving—they helped keep people warm by spinning thread that could be woven into cloth.

Before there were big clothing factories, a spinner had to spin yarn so a weaver could turn it into cloth. Then a tailor made the cloth into a cozy warm coat for when the weather turned cold.

At first, spinners used a stick with a hook on one end and a weight on the other. They attached the fleece to the hook and spun the stick. This pulled out the woolly fibers and twisted them together to make yarn.

It's called a spindle. It works, but it takes a long time.

The yarn is made from my fleece. Happy to help!

Spinning wheels were invented around 1,500 years ago. They were much faster than spinning by hand. There are different types, but they all work in a similar way: the spinner operates a treadle (foot pedal) to turn the wheel, which pulls the sheep's fleece from the spinner's hand and makes it into yarn.

All kinds of yarn can be made with a spinning wheel, including cotton and linen, which are made from cotton and flax plants.

It takes a while to learn, but now I'm superfast!

Later, steam-powered spinning machines were invented. These worked hundreds of times faster than individual spinning wheels, so huge amounts of yarn could be produced very quickly.

Ancient Spinners
There was spinning in Greek mythology. The three Fates were goddesses who controlled human lives—one spun the thread of life, one measured it out, and one cut it.

19

Color Wheels

There's one type of wheel that can help you decorate your bedroom, paint a picture, or decide what to wear.

Artists and designers use color wheels to help choose which colors to use in their work. Most color wheels have twelve sections, with a different color in each one. There are three primary colors—normally red, yellow, and blue—which can't be made from any other color. Secondary and tertiary colors are made by mixing other colors together.

The color wheel can be divided into "warm" (top) and "cool" (bottom) colors.

3
PRIMARY
COLORS

3
PRIMARY
COLORS
+3
SECONDARY
COLORS

The famous scientist Isaac Newton made a spinning color wheel that showed how different colors of light mix together.

3
PRIMARY COLORS
+ 3
SECONDARY COLORS
+ 6
TERTIARY COLORS

If you pick two colors on the wheel that are next to each other, mix them together, and paint where the two colors meet, you'll get an in-between color. You can make as many as you like—if you have a big enough wheel!

Colors opposite one another on the wheel make the biggest contrast—useful when you want to make words or pictures stand out. Other good color combinations are any three evenly spaced colors, or two colors next to one another on the wheel with the two colors opposite them.

I'm using a color from the opposite side of the wheel to make Monty's yellow fur stand out.

Woof!

All colors have tints, shades, and tones: a tint is a color mixed with white, a shade is a color mixed with black, and a tone is a color mixed with gray.

Ships' Wheels

⚓ ⚓ ⚓

Sometimes things that float need wheels. These wheels are used to steer huge ships on the high seas.

Turning the wheel moves the ship's rudder, which is like a giant oar at the back of the ship underneath the water.

Just like cart wheels, a ship's wheel has an axle that goes through the center, which controls the rudder. Handles around the outside of the wheel make it easy to control.

If I turn the wheel to the starboard, the ship moves to the right. Look out!

On a ship, "starboard" means right and "port" means left!

The ship travels in the direction that the wheel is turned. But the wheel turns the rudder in the opposite direction, because pushing the rudder to the right makes the ship move to the left, and pushing it to the left makes the ship move right.

Some ships have a double wheel—two wheels connected to each other. This allows two people to steer the ship in a storm, when one person alone might not be strong enough.

The ships' wheel was invented around the beginning of the 1700s. Before then, ships steered using a tiller—a wooden rod that moves the rudder.

squawk!

Cars Without Wheels

The first cars used tillers, until everybody realized that steering wheels made cars easier to control. The idea probably came from the ships' wheel.

Trains

Wheels that run on tracks are a great way to transport people and things. Trains pulled by locomotives have been chugging along for more than 200 years.

Rocket was an early steam-powered locomotive. It pulled trains on the world's first intercity railroad, between Liverpool and Manchester in England. The steam engine was connected to the big front wheels, and the smaller wheels at the back kept *Rocket* on the tracks.

Most of today's trains are powered by electricity or diesel, and some can go extremely fast. Japan's "bullet trains." which appeared in the 1960s, were the very first high-speed trains. Today, high-speed trains run in many countries.

LNER

Freight trains are made to transport goods. They can be over 4 miles (7 kilometers) long and might need more than one locomotive to pull them.

In the United States, steam locomotives mostly used wood as fuel. The sparks that flew out of the stacks sometimes set fire to the countryside!

In the 1930s, the streamlined *Mallard* set the world speed record for a steam locomotive—126 miles (203 kilometers) per hour.

The world train speed record is held by a French TGV train. It reached 357 miles (575 kilometers) per hour.

It wasn't long before trains went underground. The first underground railway opened in 1863 in London, England, and now there are around 180 in cities around the world.

Carousels

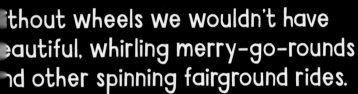

[Wi]thout wheels we wouldn't have [b]eautiful, whirling merry-go-rounds [a]nd other spinning fairground rides.

[Lo]ng before there were carousels, [kni]ghts used to practice their skills [by] playing a game on wooden [ho]rses suspended from a pole, [tur]ned by a real horse or people. [Fro]m the 1700s onward, carousels [we]re built just for fun, but they still [ne]eded animal or human power.

Carousels became really popular after steam-powered rides were invented. People whooshed around on beautifully carved, painted wooden horses at fairgrounds all over the world.

TICKETS

The base of a carousel is a big wheel turned on its side— the spinning axle in the middle turns the wheel using a system of pulleys and gears.

More gears make the horses go up and down as the carousel spins.

You can find all kinds of carousel animals, including tigers, giraffes, and pigs. There's an insect-only carousel at the Bronx Zoo in New York City, where you can ride on a praying mantis or a dung beetle.

Many fairground rides are based on the same idea as carousels. In swing rides, passengers sit in chairs attached to chains, which swing out in a circle at up to 43 miles (69 kilometers) per hour, high above the ground, as the ride spins. Playground merry-go-rounds are simple, human-powered carousels.

A **loud** pipe organ plays automatically as the carousel turns.

Pardon?

Paintings, mirrors, music, and the gorgeous horses help make the carousel experience magical.

It's tricky to get on, difficult to get off and hard to ride without falling off.

Whoooaaaa!!

The High-Wheel Bicycle

High-wheel bicycles were the first machines to be called bicycles. They're one of the world's oddest uses of wheels.

High-wheel bicycles could reach speeds of up to 25 miles (40 kilometers) per hour. They were fast because the big front wheel covered a lot of ground at each turn of the pedals.

The front wheel could measure almost 6.5 feet (2 meters) across.

These strange-looking bikes, which were also called penny-farthings, whizzed along very fast. There were a lot of bad accidents—high-wheel bicycles were hard to control, riders had a long way to fall, and there were no brakes. Even so, these bikes were popular for about 20 years in the 1870s and 1880s.

The high-wheel bicycle was replaced by the "safety bicycle" toward the end of the 1800s, and cycling became far less dangerous. This new invention had wheels of equal size, and the pedals powered a chain attached to the back wheel.

Going downhill on a high-wheel bicycle was especially challenging. Riders put their legs over the handlebars and hoped to land on their feet if they fell off.

Pennies and Farthings

The name penny-farthing came about because of two coins that were in use at the time in Great Britain: a penny was a large coin, and a farthing was a much smaller one. The bikes were also called ordinaries (even though they weren't).

Aaaargh!!

1
The first powered cart was built by Nicolas-Joseph Cugnot in 1769. It was powered by steam, so it was enormous, heavy, and slow.

Steam Cars to Driverless Cars

Wheels were doing an excellent job of getting people around. But horses can only go so far and so fast, and people began to think of other ways to get wheels moving.

During the twentieth century, cars began to sell in their millions after Henry Ford's factory in Michigan made cheap, easy-to-run cars. His most famous was the Model T.

A Model T Ford could be made in about 90 minutes!

4

5
In the middle of the twentieth century, gasoline was cheap and there was plenty of it, so cars became huge and extravagant.

Check out these wheels!

2 *I'll have you know that I also electrified the London Underground and the Blackpool streetcars in England.*

Some early cars used electric motors, like this one made by Thomas Parker in 1884.

The internal combustion engine, fueled by gasoline or diesel, became the most popular way to power cars. The first motor car with an engine was made by German engineer Karl Benz. His wife and business partner, Bertha Benz, made the world's first long-distance car journey in it.

3 *On the 125-mile (200-kilometer) trip I used my hatpin to clear a fuel line, and invented brake linings!*

6 Burning gasoline and diesel pollutes the air and contributes to climate change, so companies have started to make electric cars again. The idea is that they're powered by electricity made using energy from the Sun, or in other sustainable ways.

All of these cars need a driver. But eventually cars that can drive themselves will take over our roads. They'll be much safer than cars with human drivers.

Roller-Coasters

If you like hurtling along upside down at 15 miles (240 kilometers) per hour, you have yet another reason to be glad about wheels.

Stop! I left my stomach behind! Aaaaah!!

In Russia 500 years ago, brave riders whizzed down steep ice slides on sleds or wheeled carts. The idea reached France, where it isn't as cold, so waxed wooden slides were used instead of icy ones—the very first roller-coasters.

In the United States, people in need of excitement paid to ride on a steep railroad used for delivering coal. Later, America's first real roller-coaster, the Switchback Railway, was built. The idea soon spread all over the world.

Most roller-coasters are made from steel.

Three Wheels

Modern roller-coasters have three types of wheels. The wheels that go on top of the track make the roller-coaster whiz along. The underneath and side wheels keep the roller-coaster on the tracks.

Roller-coasters continue to get bigger, faster, and more stomach-churning . . .

- Formula Rossa, in the United Arab Emirates, is the fastest roller-coaster, at 150 miles (240 kilometers) per hour.
- Kingda Ka, in New Jersey, is the tallest at 456 feet (139 meters). Riders plummet 418 feet (127 meters) during the ride.
- Steel Dragon 2000, in Japan, is the longest roller-coaster, at 8,133 feet (2,479 meters).

In some languages, roller-coasters are called "Russian mountains."

Today there are more than 4,600 roller-coasters in the world!

Wheeeeee!!

Ferris Wheels

Ferris wheels are enormous, exciting, and absolute marvels of engineering.

Ferris wheels are named after George Ferris, who designed a huge, passenger-carrying wheel for the World's Fair in Chicago, in 1893. The giant wheel was popular—more than a million passengers enjoyed the bird's-eye view from the top—and it earned $736,000 (equal to about $20 million today) in ticket sales. Sadly, George didn't profit from his invention, and died poor.

You get a **great** view from up here!

The original Ferris wheel was 264 feet (80.4 meters) high and had 36 wooden cars. Each car carried up to 60 passengers.

The axle weighed 45 tons and was the **biggest single piece of steel** ever made at the time.

The first Ferris wheel had fallen into disrepair by 1906. Dismantling it involved blowing it up with dynamite!

George Ferris's wheel wasn't a completely new idea. In Bulgaria in the 1600s, a wooden wheel with seats for passengers was turned by a very strong man, and there were similar fairground rides after that. None of them sound especially thrilling. But the Ferris wheel was enormous, made of steel, and the first to be really fun.

There have been many more Ferris wheels since 1893. Today, the biggest one is twice the size of the original— the High Roller in Las Vegas, Nevada, stands at 550 feet (167 meters) tall.

Ferris wheels are extremely difficult and expensive to make. Much to everyone's disappointment, several Ferris wheels have been planned but abandoned partway through.

Bicycles

Bicycles are an excellent way to travel because they keep you in shape, don't pollute the atmosphere, and convert human energy into movement more efficiently than anything else ever invented! There are so many kinds.

BMX, short for bicycle motocross, began as a pedal-power version of off-road motorcycling. BMX riders can perform amazing jumps and other stunts.

There are more than one billion bikes in the world, speeding people along on everyday trips.

Whoooaaaa!!

Mountain bikes are good for off-road adventures. They have fatter tires for rough ground and low gears for steep hills.

Roller Skates and Skateboards

Roller skates and skateboards provide some of the best fun it is possible to have on wheels.

People have been whizzing around with wheels attached to their feet since the 1700s. The first roller skates were almost impossible to turn or stop, but better designs made roller skating safer and much more popular.

A roller-skating craze swept the United States in the 1860s and 1870s and spread to Europe. Since then, roller skating has never gone out of fashion.

Whiz!!

Zoom!!

People use skates as a fast and fun way to get around, but they also compete in roller-skating sports, including speed skating, roller hockey, and dancing. In the sport of Roller Derby, teams of skaters zoom around a rink in a fast and furious race, blocking the opposing team, slamming into one another, and sending players flying.

In the middle of the twentieth century, skateboards were invented in California. Because California is also famous for surfing, skateboarding used to be known as sidewalk surfing.

What you **really** need are wings!

If you need an excuse to jump on a skateboard, June 21 is Go Skateboarding Day.

You can use a skateboard to get you to school or to the grocery store but skateboarders often learn tricks as well. An "ollie" is one of the most basic tricks—lifting the board into the air while you're riding it. Once you've spent weeks mastering an ollie, you'll have the basis for all kinds of other moves.

There are thousands of skate parks around the world where you can demonstrate your tricks. The biggest is in Guangzhou, China—it covers an area the size of 65 tennis courts.

Race Cars

⊚ ⊚ ⊚ ⊚ ⊚

There are many different styles of motor racing, with different types of cars and tracks. But they all have one thing in common: the cars zoom along at alarming speeds. Two of the fastest and most popular kinds of motor racing in the world are NASCAR and Formula 1, in which cars reach speeds of more than 211 miles (340 kilometers) per hour!

Once wheels had engines attached to them, they were really good at going fast. Hardly any time at all after the first cars were made, people started racing them.

In the United States, NASCAR stands for the National Association for Stock Car Auto Racing. The cars look a lot like ordinary cars, but they're lightning-fast. The most famous race is the Daytona 500, run over 500 miles (800 kilometers) in 200 laps around the Daytona International Speedway in Florida.

Race car drivers need excellent vision, coordination, and reaction speeds . . . .

Formula 1 motor racing is an international competition, with fans around the world. The "formula" is a set of rules governing the size of the cars, engines, wheels, and so on, that all the cars have to follow. One of the most famous races is the Monaco Grand Prix, where the cars screech around 78 laps of the streets of the city of Monte Carlo. There are other "Formula" races, too, including Formula E for electric cars.

In the United States, IndyCar racing has millions of fans. The cars look similar to Formula 1 cars, with their wheels outside the body of the car, and go just as fast.

Really, Really Big Wheels

⬤ ⬤ ⬤ ⬤ ⬤

These are some of the biggest vehicles in the world—and of course they need really big wheels to move them around.

Monster trucks are famous for being huge. The biggest one of all is called Bigfoot. It weighs as much as three African elephants, it's taller than an 18-wheeler, and its tires measure 10 feet (3 meters) across.

> There's a longer monster truck—it's a monster limousine—that's almost 30 feet (10 meters) long. But it's nowhere near as impressive!

BIGFOOT

This truck is not designed to go on roads—it's far too big!—but it does have an engine and can be driven. Anyone for a spin?

Even bigger than Bigfoot is the biggest pickup truck in the world. This replica of a Dodge Power Wagon has a house inside it! It's about eight times as big as the original Dodge truck, weighs 55 tons and includes a living room, a kitchen, four bedrooms, and a bathroom.

Road hog!

Normal-size
Dodge Power Wagon

But the biggest pickup truck is just a baby compared to the largest land vehicle in the world. The giant bucket wheel excavator is a mining vehicle that works in a German coal mine. This immense vehicle also uses another wheel for digging—the bucket wheel at the front measures 70 feet (21 meters) across.

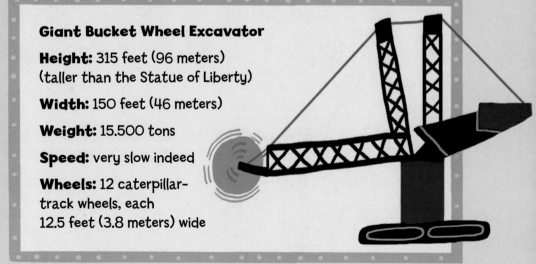

Giant Bucket Wheel Excavator

Height: 315 feet (96 meters)
(taller than the Statue of Liberty)

Width: 150 feet (46 meters)

Weight: 15,500 tons

Speed: very slow indeed

Wheels: 12 caterpillar-track wheels, each 12.5 feet (3.8 meters) wide

Wheel of Fortune

This imaginary wheel comes from ancient mythology and belongs to a goddess. It shows how easily human fortunes can change.

Who knows when I might feel like giving it a spin? **Whoops!**

The goddess Fortuna spins her wheel at random— she's supposed not to know or care how her wheel affects people. It means good luck if the wheel turns and someone finds themselves at the top, but for the person opposite them at the bottom of the wheel, it means bad luck. In medieval times, the person at the top was usually represented by a king.

Someone at the height of wealth and happiness might be spun down to misery and poverty, or the other way around. **Whoa!**

The zodiac is usually shown as a wheel, too: it's a collection of twelve star constellations through which the Sun passes over the course of a year. Just as medieval people believed that the Wheel of Fortune affected their lives, some people believe that the zodiac affects them—they think that the positions of the Sun, Moon, and planets can change what happens in people's lives.

Here we go again!

Today, the Wheel of Fortune is better known as a television game show! Contestants solve word puzzles, while spinning a giant wheel to rack up cash prizes. The show began in the 1970s, and it's still on TV today.

Time Line

Climb aboard our superfast time machine for a quick spin through the history of wheels.

Around 4500 B.C.

Potters' wheels were the first wheels ever invented.

Around 1300s

The first mechanical clocks, using cogs and other wheels, were invented.

A.D. Around 500

Spinning wheels were invented, so making textiles and clothes became a lot quicker.

1666

Isaac Newton developed the world's first color wheel.

Around 1700

People used ships' wheels to steer ships for the first time.

1884

The first roller-coaster, the Switchback Railway, thrilled fair-goers at Coney Island. It was designed by LaMarcus Adna Thompson.

1893

The first Ferris wheel, named after inventor George Ferris, spun around in Chicago.

1872

The internal combustion engine was invented by George Brayton in the United States.

1940s or 1950s

The first skateboards were invented in California.

Around 3500 B.C.

The earliest wheels on a vehicle date from 3500 B.C.

Around 2000 B.C.

The first chariots, which had spoked wheels, were pulled into battle by horses.

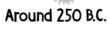

Around 250 B.C.

Gears were used for predicting positions of the Sun and Moon in a machine made in ancient Greece.

Around 300 B.C.

The first waterwheels were used—the first machines to use something other than human or animal power.

1802

The first railroad steam locomotive was invented by Richard Trevithick in England.

1861

The first steam-powered carousel was invented in England by Thomas Bradshaw.

1869

The high-wheel bicycle was invented by French engineer Eugène Meyer.

1863

The first underground railway, powered by steam, opened in London, England.

1980s

The first driverless cars were developed.

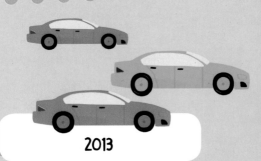

2013

Four U.S. states allowed driverless cars on public roads—the first in the world.

INDEX

48

Now that you know all about wheels, look out for a book about wings!

WITHDRAWN

31901065165831